THE
EVERYTHING

DREAMS
MINI BOOK

Understand the
messages from your mind

Trish and Rob MacGregor

Adams Media Corporation
Holbrook, Massachusetts

An Everything Series Book.
"Everything" is a trademark of Adams Media Corporation.

Published by Adams Media Corporation
260 Center Street, Holbrook, MA 02343
www.adamsmedia.com

ISBN: 1-58062-386-7

Printed in Canada.

J I H G F E D C B A

Library of Congress Cataloging-in-Publication Data
available from the publisher.

This publication is designed to provide accurate and authoritative information with
regard to the subject matter covered. It is sold with the understanding that the publisher is not engaged in rendering legal, accounting, or other professional advice. If
legal advice or other expert assistance is required, the services of a competent professional person should be sought.

— From a *Declaration of Principles* jointly adopted by a Committee of the
American Bar Association and a Committee of Publishers and Associations

Cover illustrations by Barry Littmann.
Interior illustrations by Barry Littmann and Kathie Kelleher.

This book is available at quantity discounts for bulk purchases.
For information, call 1-800-872-5627.

Contents

 **Introduction**

Almost everyone has awakened from a startling dream and wondered for a few moments what it meant, and then forgotten about it as the day's activities began. But the residue of the dream clings to you. Was there a message in it for you?

Now imagine another scenario. You wake in the morning from the same dream, but this time you remember it in its entirety. You jot it down, then interpret it, and realize it addresses some of the major concerns in your life.

Most dream researchers agree that we all can use our dreams as tools for better understanding ourselves, for dealing with and solving our waking-life problems, or even as a way of increasing our creativity and productivity. We can use them to enhance relationships, gain insight about a health problem, obtain career guidance, or even find a new town to live in.

By following the instructions for recalling, recording, and interpreting dreams, you can avoid letting your dreams slip away from you, and gain a new perspective on your life. Even if you already recall and record dreams, you'll discover new ways for interpreting and understanding them. With practice, you can learn how to program dreams and adventure into new worlds, meet both friends and intriguing strangers, and even search past lives and get a peek at future events.

EXERCISE 1: SLEEP HABITS

Use this exercise to track your sleep habits for two weeks. Note the time you went to sleep, approximately how long it took you to go to sleep, the time you woke up, how you felt, whether you were rested, whether you napped in the afternoon, and anything else that pertains to your sleep patterns. This will prepare you for the dream work you'll be doing later in this book.

Sunday

Bedtime: _____ Awake Time: _____

Comments: _____

_____

_____

Monday

Bedtime: _____ Awake Time: _____

Comments: _____

_____

_____

Tuesday

Bedtime: _____ Awake Time: _____

Comments: _____

_____

_____

(continued)

EXERCISE 1: SLEEP HABITS

Wednesday

Bedtime: _____ Awake Time: _____

Comments: _____

_____

_____

Thursday

Bedtime: _____ Awake Time: _____

Comments: _____

_____

_____

Friday

Bedtime: _____ Awake Time: _____

Comments: _____

_____

_____

Saturday

Bedtime: _____ Awake Time: _____

Comments: _____

_____

_____

Chapter One
Remembering Dreams

To catch your dream, have pen and paper or a tape recorder next to your bed— a material suggestion.

— SHEILA OSTRANDER AND LYNN SCHROEDER

Sometimes, dreams are so startling or vivid that you come awake during the night.

At that time, you might think, *I won't forget this one.* Yet, by morning a fog may settle over your memories of the night's "events" and you may only recall the flavor of the dream and little else. Or, you may just remember thinking that you weren't going to forget your dream.

The best way to remember dreams is to record them immediately after they occur. If you don't usually wake up after a dream, try giving yourself a suggestion before you go to sleep that you will wake up following each dream, although it might not be a good idea to do so every night. You may reach a point where you can recall four or five or more dreams a night.

Either jot down the dream on a bedside pad or record it on a tape. If you decide to write down the dream, you can either use a penlight or learn to write in the dark. At first, your night-time scrawls may be virtually inde-cipherable, but with practice you can write clearly enough so that you will be able to transcribe the dream into a journal in the morning.

The next best time to recall a dream is in the morning before you get up. The experts all seem to agree that how you awaken in the morning is vital to preliminary recall of dreams. If you can dispense with an alarm clock, by all means do so. An alarm intrudes, jerking you from a sound sleep so quickly that your dream tends to fade as soon as you open your eyes.

To awaken without an alarm, of course, is difficult if you're working a nine-to-five job or have young children. One alternative is to start your dream work on a weekend, when you may be able to sleep later and to wake up without an alarm. Another alternative is to train yourself to wake up without an alarm. This is actually much easier to do than it sounds. Before going to sleep at night, simply give yourself a suggestion to wake up at a particular time, say, ten minutes before your alarm clock goes off. If it doesn't work immediately, keep trying until you feel confident you can eliminate the alarm clock.

Once you wake up, don't open your eyes. Just lie there for a few minutes, retrieving your dream images. If nothing comes to mind, move into your favorite sleep position. This may trigger some dream fragment that will expand.

"For some as yet unknown reason," writes Patricia Garfield in her book *Creative Dreaming*, "additional dream recall often comes when you move gently from one position and settle into another."

At first, you may remember only bits and pieces, an image, a word, a face. But with practice, large parts of your last dream will come to you. These parts, in turn, may trigger a memory of the dream before it. Eventually, this process will become automatic, as intrinsic to your morning ritual as brushing your teeth.

Sometimes it helps to have reference points to aid you in the recollection of a dream.

Quite often, our own thoughts about our dreams are the biggest obstacles to recalling them. A dream may be so unusual that you wake up certain that you'll remember it, only to forget it within minutes of opening your eyes. On the other hand, you might think a dream is too silly or embarrassing to write down, or that it's not worth remembering.

It's best to avoid making value judgments about a dream and simply write it down as if it were someone else's story. Later, when you interpret the dream, you may find that what seemed silly or outrageous or insignificant has far deeper meaning than you initially realized.

The Dream Journal

A dream journal is an integral part of dream exploration, a portal to other parts of yourself that is rather like the hole Alice fell through on her way to Wonderland. A notebook will do, but a bound journal is even better. Many bookstores now sell bound journals with blank pages inside. Some are specifically designed as dream journals and include a place for the date and time of the dream, the dream itself, and your interpretation.

If your bedside writing isn't clear, transcribe your dreams later into a "per-  manent" notebook or onto a computer file. If you use a notebook computer, keep it near the bed and type the dreams directly into it when you wake up.

Keep the journal and a penlight nearby— on a nightstand, on the floor, or even under your pillow. If you jot down your dreams during the night or tape record them, then set aside a time to transcribe them into your journal.

When you describe the dream, include as many details as possible. The interrogatives—

who, what, where, when, and how—
act as excellent guidelines in collecting
details. Were you alone? If not, who was with
you? Friends? Family? Strangers? What
activity, if any, were you or the others
engaged in? Was it day or night? Dark or light?
Where were you? How did the dream "feel" to
you? Familiar? Odd? Pleasant?

Brugh Joy attributes particular significance to the lighting in a dream. If a dream
is brilliantly colored and very vivid, it
reflects what he calls the "superconscious"
state, the more evolved
areas of consciousness.
In his own life, these
types of dreams are
nearly always
prophetic. If the
light in a dream is
soft or shadowy, in

sepia tones like an old photograph, or if it's in black and white, Joy says it emanates from less evolved areas of consciousness. Dreams that are even darker originate from the deep unconscious. When you record a dream, one of the details that should be included is how you felt upon awakening. What is your dominant emotion? Exhilaration? Fear? Sadness? Happiness? Sometimes, when you go over the dream later, you may remember more details.

Montague Ullman advises that when you record a dream, jot down whatever you were thinking about when you went to bed. It may provide a clue to the meaning of the dream.

Sometimes, you may not remember the specifics of a dream, but only that you've dreamed. Then, later that day or several days later, your recollection of the dream is triggered by something in your waking environment. Be sure to note the event or experience that triggered the recollection, because it may provide vital clues about the dream's meaning or significance.

If you're not getting enough sleep, recalling your dreams is going to be much more difficult. Refer to the exercise in the introduction on sleep habits to refresh your memory about how much sleep you need and readjust your schedule accordingly. You may want to note in your journal how long you sleep on a given night and how many

EXERCISE 2: DREAM JOURNAL

Here is a sample page from a dream journal. Use this merely as a starting point and feel free to add to it and change it as you like. The beauty of dream work is that it's an empirical process, and we are all pioneers. Use these following pages for one full week and see if there is a difference in the way you remember your dreams.

Date: _____ Time: _____

Presleep thoughts: _____

_____

Dream: _____

_____

Interpretation: _____

_____

Feelings upon waking: _____

_____

Additional comments: _____

_____

times you wake up. If you habitually wake up at night, try taking advantage of the situation by seeing if you can recall any dreams. If you do, then record them. If you initially have trouble recalling dreams at night, then try recapturing a dream when you wake up from a nap. This works well for some people.

Meditation and Dream Recall

Meditation can be another means to help you recall dreams. The process makes you aware of other states of mind, and ultimately may enhance your recollection of dreams. By quieting your conscious mind, symbols and images are allowed to flow more freely from the intuitive self.

The technique you use depends entirely on what feels most natural to you. A walk in the woods or on the beach can serve your

purpose just as well as ten or twenty minutes of sitting quietly after you wake up.
Orloff meditates every morning in front of
an altar that contains objects that hold special meaning for her. When she misses a
day, she says, she feels less centered.

EXERCISE 3: RECALLING A DREAM

This provides a list of points to look for in recalling a dream.

1. What was the location of the dream?

   Was it indoors or outdoors? Above ground or below ground?

   Was it located in a familiar or an unfamiliar place?

   Was it located in another town or city?

2. Were there people involved?

   Did you know them or were they strangers?

   Were they in your life now or from your past?

   Were any of them celebrities?

3. What emotions were involved?

   Were you exhilarated, happy, afraid, depressed, confused, or lonely?

   Did your emotional state change during the dream? If so, what caused the change?

4. Were there any animals in the dream?

   Were they friendly, fierce looking, gentle, or wise?

5. What objects or symbols were involved in the dream?

6. What was said in the dream?

   Did anyone in the dream speak directly to you? What was said?

7. What was the major action in the dream?

Chapter Two

Dream Incubation

We're constantly guided by our dreams, whether we remember them or not. But once you begin to recall dreams with ease, it's possible to request dreams that will guide you and even give you hints of future events on particular issues or dilemmas. It might be a relationship issue, a health matter, a career question, or something else. Or you may simply request a dream that you will remember. The act of asking for a dream, for whatever purpose, is called dream incubation.

This process was popular in many ancient cultures including Mesopotamia, ancient Egypt, Rome, and Greece. People often traveled to temples dedicated to specific gods, where they spent the night in hopes of receiving a dream that would heal, illuminate, guide, and provide solutions.

In some temples, priests were available to help seekers interpret their dreams. There were even professional dream seekers, who were hired by people too ill or otherwise unable to travel to the dream temples. Those who participated usually were required to undergo fasts, baths, or other rituals.

Today, there may be no recognized dream temples for seekers, but anyone can practice dream incubation in their own home. The first step in dream incubation is knowing what to ask for. Are you concerned about a health problem? A career move? Your family?

The Method

After considering what you've written, pick one of the areas and select a concern. Now you are ready to begin practicing dream incubation.

Some experts recommend writing your request for a dream on a slip of paper and placing it on your nightstand or under your pillow. The idea is that by making it a ritual, you are formalizing it. But most of the time, a sincere need and intent will suffice. And, of course, you have to remember the dream. But even the need to remember the dream can be included in your request.

Gayle Delaney, in her book *Breakthrough Dreaming,* suggests that you jot down five or ten  lines about your request in your dream journal. Then condense this to a phrase or question that states what you want to know. Fall asleep repeating this phrase or question to yourself.

Even if you don't remember anything the first time you try this, keep at it. With persistence, you'll recall a dream that addresses your concern. Some of your answers, however, may not be what you bargained for.

The brainstorming exercise is intended to help you identify areas of your life that you would like to change. Once you recognize them, you'll have a better idea about what to request from your dreaming self.

1. Relationships

☆ My most intimate relationships are generally . . .

☆ I don't understand why my spouse or significant other . . .

☆ I feel good about my relationship with . . .

because . . .

☆ I would like to change my relationship with . . .

because . . .

☆ I would like to end my relationship with . . .

because . . .

☆ The pattern in my intimate relationships is . . .

☆ My relationship with my parents is . . .

because . . .

☆ My relationship with my brothers or sisters is . . .

because . . .

☆ If possible, I would change . . .

☆ I am happiest in relationships that . . .

☆ In a perfect world, my relationships would . . .

2. Work/career

☆ I . . . . . . my job.

☆ With my work/job/career, I would like to change . . .

☆ My ideal job/career is . . .

☆ I would like to be earning . . .

☆ I . . . . my boss.

☆ I don't get along with . . .

☆ In terms of work/career, my bliss would be . . .

3. Health/physical self

I like . . . . /don't like . . . . the way I look/feel.

☆ If I could change anything about the way I look, it would be . . .

☆ My health is . . .

☆ I have a chronic problem with . . .

(continued)

EXERCISE 4: DREAM INCUBATION

☆ I have been to . . . doctors in the last six months.

☆ I have missed . . . days of work in the last six months.

☆ My ideal physical self would be . . .

4. **Spiritual life**

   ☆ I believe in . . .

   ☆ I feel. . . . . about my spiritual life.

   ☆ In my spiritual life, I would like to develop . . .

   ☆ I would like to change . . .

   ☆ I would like to experience . . .

5. **Life in general**

   ☆ In six months I would like to be . . .

   ☆ In a year, I would like to be . . .

   ☆ Within five years, I envision myself . . .

6. **I need guidance on:**

Chapter Three

Dream Interpretations

When you first begin interpreting symbols and themes in your dreams, work with your own dream symbols first, rather than immediately turning to this glossary. Take note of details in your dreams—colors, vividness, the action, or anything unusual that stands out. If you dream of a particular animal, for instance, associate it with situations and conditions in your life, institutions that you deal with, or people you know well.

When it comes to dreams, there are no universal rules or meanings. Keep that in mind when you use this glossary. Also, note that some dreams might be a literal message of something that is about to happen to you, rather than a symbolic message. A dream scenario might also relate to scenes from a past life. Although such interpretations might be rare, they are worth considering.

A

Abdomen Seeing your abdomen in a dream suggests the gestation or digestion of a new idea or phase of your life. If your abdomen is swollen, the birth of a new project may be imminent.

Actor or Actress Perhaps you're only seeing your own or someone else's persona, the side the person shows to the world.

Seeing yourself as an actor in the spotlight suggests a desire for publicity or a more public life. Such a dream can also suggest that you're acting out a role or "putting on an act" for someone else.

Afternoon Dreams that take place in the afternoon suggest clarity and lengthiness of duration. Are you with friends in the afternoon? Then positive and lasting associations may soon be formed.

Airplane You may be soaring to new heights in some facet of your life or taking a metaphorical journey into the unconscious. An airplane dream can also be a prelude to a flying dream or used as a launch pad to a lucid dream.

Alligator This symbol may suggest that you're being thick-skinned or insensitive to someone else. It may also signify danger.

Amusement Park Dreaming of an amusement park may suggest that you are in need of a vacation from your concerns over a troubling issue. To dream of riding a ride denotes an enjoyment of life and feelings of being uninhibited.

Anchor An anchor grounds you—acts as your foundation. It also holds you in place, which can be either beneficial or detrimental.

Angels Angels represent help from the higher self or from a guardian. The appearance of an angel may suggest a growing spiritual awareness.

Animals Animals can relate to various sides of your "animal" nature, a guardian spirit, wisdom, innocence, predatory tendencies, or sexuality, depending on the perceived nature of the animal. An animal can also represent the physical body, or appear as a metaphor for an illness within the physical body.

Ant Ants suggest restlessness (feeling "antsy"). They also signify small annoyances and irritations. Alternately, they may represent feelings of smallness or insignificance. Consider the number of ants in the dream. Is it a single ant? A colony? Or a huge, swollen anthill?

Apparition An apparition can signify a message or warning. It can be seen as communication with the dead. Alternately, you might feel that another person in a relationship is like an apparition—someone who is there, but not truly present.

Apples Apples stand for wholeness and for knowledge. Ripe apples on a tree may mean that your hope and hard work have borne fruit.

April As April showers lead to May flowers, to dream of this month represents that much pleasure and fortune may be heading your way. If the weather is bad, it may suggest the passing of bad luck.

Arch Passing under an arch in a dream may symbolize a transition in your life, a move from one phase or stage to another. If you avoid walking under the arch, the indication is that you are resisting transition or change. Note the shape of the arch, whether it's adorned in any way, or whether other people are also using it. This will flesh out the symbol for you.

Arm Arms allow you to manipulate things in your environment. The same might be true in a dream. Seeing an arm suggests that you can maneuver or manipulate things in your dream environment. If you flap your arms, it may indicate a desire to fly in your dream.

Atlas Dreaming of an atlas suggests that you are considering moving or taking a trip.

Attic If you dream of entering an attic, you may be exploring the realm of the higher self or seeking knowledge there. An attic can also suggest a place where things are hidden or stored from the past. The dream might be suggesting that you take some part of you out of hiding or that you should dispose of the things you are clinging to from your past.

August Dreaming of August may suggest unfortunate dealings in business and love. A young woman dreaming that she will be wed in this month is an omen of sorrow in her early married life.

B

Baby A baby in a dream may represent an idea that is gestating or growing. It could also relate to the pending birth of a child or a desire for a family. Alternately, a baby could indicate dependent behavior or infantile longings. A baby walking alone indicates independence. A bright, clean baby represents requited love and many warm friends.

Bells

Dreaming of bells tolling means a distant friend will die. If you dream of a joyous bell ringing, however, expect success in all aspects of your life.

If you dream of an alarm ringing in warning, it indicates you have worries about some aspect of your life. If you dream you hear a doorbell ringing, expect to be called away to visit a friend or relative in need.

Balcony A balcony might stand for the public part of the personality. Consider the condition of the balcony. If it's clean and polished, the dream indicates that you are held in high regard by others. If it's a crumbling, tarnished balcony, it may suggest that you need to repair your public image.

Bank Generally, a bank is a symbol of security and power—a foundation—but the meaning depends on what you're doing in the bank. If you are receiving or depositing money, it's usually an auspicious sign, an indication that you are financially secure. If you are waiting in line, it literally may mean waiting for a check or money to arrive. Likewise, if you're holding up a bank, it may symbolize that money

you're expecting is being "held up" or delayed.

Basement Dreaming of being in a basement could indicate that you are connecting with the subconscious mind. Possibly you are unearthing something hidden in your past that you need to examine. (see Underground.)

Bathroom Dreaming of being in a bathroom could simply mean that your bladder is full. It could also symbolize a place of privacy. If the bathroom is crowded, the dream could mean that you lack privacy. If you find yourself in a bathroom for the opposite sex, it may suggest that you are crossing boundaries. A bathroom dream may also relate to the elimination of something in your life.

Birds The appearance of a bird in a dream could relate to a wish for freedom, to fly away, or to flee from something. Birds can also be spiritual symbols. Among certain Native American tribes, an eagle symbolizes spiritual knowledge. A vulture might symbolize death and a hummingbird might point to a matter accelerating or to the tendency to flit from one thing to another.

Birthday Birthday dreams can have contrary meanings depending on the context. To dream of receiving birthday presents may mean happy surprises or advancements are in order. For an older person to dream of a birthday may signify long hardship and sorrow; to the young it is a symbol of poverty.

Bleeding Blood is vital to life, and to dream of bleeding suggests a loss of power and a change for the worse in fortune.

Birds of Prey

There is a scheming person out to injure you if you dream of vultures. But this evildoer will not succeed if you dream the vulture is dead. A woman dreaming of a vulture indicates she will soon be overwhelmed by slander and gossip.

If you dream of a buzzard, also watch out. An old scandal is likely to surface and injure your reputation. And if you dream of a buzzard sitting on a railroad, you might experience an accident or loss in the near future.

Should the buzzard in your dream fly away, all your troubles will be resolved!

Breasts Women's breasts may relate to sexual desire. They can also symbolize nurturing, motherhood, or a concern about exposure. Are the breasts exposed? Are they diseased or injured? Always consider what's going on in relation to the symbol.

Bridge Since a bridge connects us from one place to another, in dreaming it may represent a crossing from one state of mind to another. Consider the other elements in the dream. Are you crossing dangerous waters? What's waiting for you at the other side of the bridge? What's behind you?

Bus A bus can be a vehicle for moving ahead to one's goal. If you're traveling with others, you could be on a collective journey. Notice other aspects of the dream, such as the luggage you're carrying, your destination, and what you're leaving behind.

C

Cage A cage represents possession or control, and what you see in the cage is the key to interpreting this sign. A cage full of birds may signify great wealth and many children, while a single bird may represent a successful marriage or mate. An empty cage may mean the loss of a family member, while a cage full of wild animals may signify that you have control over a particular aspect of your life and that you will triumph over misfortune.

Cake A cake might symbolize that a celebration is at hand. Or perhaps there's something to celebrate that has been overlooked.

Canal Canals suggest a journey through the unconscious. Pay attention to other details in the dream. Is the water muddy or clear? Are you traveling with friends or family?

Cancer Dreaming of cancer doesn't mean you have it or are going to get it. To be successfully treated for cancer in a dream signals a change for the better. Dreaming of cancer may symbolize a desperate or foreboding situation, or a draining of resources.

Candles Usually something of a spiritual nature is suggested by the appearance of candles. A candle provides light in the dark, or guidance through dark matters or through the unknown. If a candle burns down to nothingness, it might indicate a fear or concern about death or impotence. A candle being put out could indicate a feeling of being overworked. A steadily burning candle may signify a steadfast character and constancy in friends and family.

Canoe Canoes suggest a short journey that requires some effort, but that is often pleasantly tranquil. Pay attention to other elements in the dream, such as the state of the water and how hard you are paddling. A dream of paddling on a calm stream symbolizes confidence in your own abilities. If the river is shallow and quick, the dream may indicate concern over a hasty decision in a recent matter. To dream of rowing with your paramour may indicate an imminent and lasting marriage, but if the waters are rough, then perhaps some effort is required before you are ready to marry.

Car A moving car may mean you are headed toward a goal or moving ahead. If you're in the driver's seat, a car can symbolize taking charge of your life. Is there a "backseat driver" in the vehicle? Or are you taking the backseat in some situation in your life? Being a passenger indicates that someone else might be controlling a situation. A stolen or lost car could indicate that you are losing control of your life. Cars sometimes represent the physical body, so take note of the car's condition. Is it rusting? Does the exterior shine? How does the interior look?

Carousel To dream of riding a carousel suggests that you are going round in circles and not making any progress in your endeavors. Seeing others ride a carousel symbolizes unfulfilled ambitions.

Castle Seeing one of these majestic structures in a dream might suggest power and strength, security and protection. Castles in the sky are fantasies and illusions, wishes to escape from one's present circumstances.

Cat Cats can have both positive and negative attributes, depending on your association with cats and the surrounding circumstances in the dream. Cats can mean prosperity; kittens can mean new ideas. Kittens in a basement could be ideas arising from the unconscious mind. Cats can represent independence, the feminine, or sexual prowess. They can also stand for evil or bad luck, or a catty or cunning person.

Cattle To dream of healthy, content cattle grazing in a green pasture suggests prosperity and happiness. Conversely, dreaming of weak, poorly fed cattle suggests you are misspending your energy. Stampeding cattle implies that something in your life is out of control.

Cellar A cellar often symbolizes the unconscious mind, a place where knowledge is stored or hidden. It can also indicate that the dream comes from the deepest levels of your unconscious, so pay special attention to the way the cellar is lit and to colors and textures.

Chariot Riding in a chariot in a dream suggests positive news or success in a matter.

Children By dreaming of children, you possibly may yearn to return to a simpler, less complicated life. Such dreams might also relate to a desire to return to the past to recapture good times or to satisfy unfulfilled hopes.

Chocolate Chocolate suggests a need or a desire to indulge in something, perhaps a forbidden something. It also can indicate a need to limit your indulgences.

Circle A circle in Jungian terms represents the Self, wholeness. It can also relate to a symbol of protection or social connections, as in a "circle" of friends. If you're "circling around something," caution is indicated. Finally, the Freudian interpretation is that the circle represents the vagina and sexual desire.

Closet Closets are places where things are stored or hidden. If there is something you are hiding in your life, your dream possibly may indicate that it is time to release whatever it is.

Clouds Dark, stormy clouds rolling in at a low altitude and flashing lightning may

Coffee & Coffeehouses

Whether it's Starbucks or Dunkin' Donuts, if you dream of drinking coffee, it denotes that your friends disapprove of your marriage intentions. That's assuming you have marriage intentions. If you are already married and you dream of drinking coffee, be prepared for many disagreements and quarrels. If you dream you are roasting coffee—does anyone know how to roast coffee?—you soon will marry a stranger. To dream of ground coffee signifies you will be successful in overcoming some adversity.

To dream of visiting a coffeehouse denotes that women are conspiring against you and your possessions. This is true if a man or woman dreams of visiting a coffeehouse.

represent your anger regarding a situation. A slate gray clouded sky might indicate that your views are clouded on a subject. What is it in your life that needs clarity? Dreaming of white, billowing clouds floating in a blue sky suggests that matters are clearing up.

Coffin A coffin may symbolize a feeling of confinement. Coffins also relate to death; ask yourself what part of your life might be dead.

College College represents distinction and the attainment of your hopes through hard work. To dream of a college may suggest that you will advance to a position long sought after. Dreaming that you are back in college suggests that distinction will follow a period of hard work.

Corpse To dream of yourself as a corpse or to experience your death is not necessarily a prediction of your demise. It could signify a major change in your life, such as the ending of a long-held job or a divorce. If you dream of killing yourself, it could mean that you are going through a traumatic personal transformation, leaving your old life behind.

Cow A cow can represent fertility, sustenance, or even prosperity. Alternately, a cow might signify a desire for sexual intercourse, or a fear of being unable to resist engaging in sex.

Creek A creek represents a short journey or a new experience. Are you exploring a creek with a friend? Is the creek muddy? Note the other aspects of the dream.

Crown The obvious definition is wealth, position, power, and authority. But is the crown something desired or feared in the dream? Is it within reach or escaping your grasp?

D

Dancing A dream dance evokes movement, freedom, joy, and a time of happiness and levity.

Darkness Darkness is a symbol of the unconscious, the hidden, and the unknown. Darkness can also stand for evil, death, and fear. To dream of being overtaken by darkness suggests fear or trepidation over a matter at hand. To dream that you lose a friend or child in the darkness symbolizes that you may be provoked from many different sources.

Daybreak Daybreaks symbolize that the outlook is brightening on a matter. A gloomy or cloudy day suggests bad luck in a new enterprise.

Dead The appearance of the dead in a dream typically signifies a warning of some kind. To see the dead living and happy represents a bad influence that may be affecting your life.

Death A death dream usually isn't a premonition of death, but it may indicate a death. If there's no sense of fear in the death, the dream can mean you're letting go of something, moving on. On the other hand, a corpse can indicate a lifeless routine.

December A time of gift giving and receiving, to dream of this month can suggest the accumulation of wealth and fortune.

Deer A deer in a dream may symbolize hunting. Deer are also graceful and gentle creatures, easily frightened. In folklore, deer are the messengers of fairies and therefore could be seen as messengers of the unconscious.

Desert A desert is usually thought of as a barren place, where little grows. It can be symbolic of a fear of death, or of being barren. But a desert can also symbolize hidden beauty and hidden life that is camouflaged to ordinary perceptions.

Dew Suggestive of tiny treasures or small pleasures, to dream of sparkling dew may represent that wealth and achievement are due. For a single person, perhaps a fortunate marriage is imminent.

Diamond A diamond symbolizes love, as in a diamond ring, and money. A lost diamond, especially a ring, may symbolize a concern about a love relationship. A gift of a diamond depends on who's giving it and other circumstances. A diamond from a parent or relative could relate to an inheritance; one from a friend might indicate a wish to obtain the person's love.

Digging What are you digging for? If it's something lost, you may be attempting to retrieve a part of your past. If it's a treasure, you may be delving into the unconscious, a treasure-house of knowledge. If, however, you are burying something, it indicates a wish to cover up an act, hide your feelings, or hide the facts of the matter.

Diving To dream of diving into a body of water may indicate that you are about to dive into something related to your waking life. On a deeper level, a diving dream may symbolize an exploration of the unconscious. From a Freudian perspective, such a dream suggests the dreamer is diving into a new sexual relationship.

Doctor A doctor can indicate a healing or healing guide. For some people, a doctor in a dream might symbolize mainstream thinking as opposed to alternative health options.

Dog Dreaming of a dog can mean that you're seeking companionship, affection, or loyalty. If the dog bites, it might indicate a feeling of disloyalty. To hear dogs barking suggests a message or a warning from your unconscious.

Dolphins A dolphin may be considered a messenger of the unconscious, since it resides in the sea. Perhaps the dolphin is a guide to the unconscious realms, which may suggest that you are diving into the unconscious.

Door A common dream symbol, doors can indicate an opening or a new opportunity at hand. A closed door suggests that something is inaccessible or hidden. If a door is broken, there may be something hindering you from the new opportunity. The condition of the door, the material it's made of, and any markings that appear on it often provide clues about what lies behind a closed door.

Drinking Drinking water in a dream might simply mean that you are thirsty.

Symbolically, water is related to the unconscious and emotions. Drinking may suggest you are being nourished or have a thirst for emotional involvement. Drinking alcoholic beverages can symbolize a sense of feeling high about a matter. As a metaphor, the drinking of "spirits" may suggest a search for spiritual sustenance. For an alcoholic or someone close to an alcoholic, a dream of drinking alcohol might be a warning.

Drought Generally an unfavorable omen in a dream, droughts represent the absence of life or the drying up of your emotions. Are you with someone in the dream? Then maybe there is an unresolved issue between you and someone you are close to that is leading to a quarrel or separation.

Drum Dreaming of a drum or drumbeats might relate to a primitive urge. Alternately, a drum possibly symbolizes communication, magic, or even an entrepreneurial spirit—as in drumming-up business.

Dusk Dusk denotes the end of the day; the end of happiness or clarity on an issue, or a dark outlook on a matter at hand.

Dwarf Dwarfs are traditionally associated with magical powers. Dreaming of a dwarf could be an extremely fortuitous sign. On the other hand, a dwarf can symbolize a stunted condition. If growth is limited, alternate paths must be pursued.

Dying Dreams of dying represent the ending of an emotional state or situation at hand. To dream that you are going to die suggests an inattention to a particular aspect of your life. To see animals in the throes of death symbolizes bad influences are a threat.

E

Eagle The eagle, soaring through the sky, can symbolize a spiritual quest. The bird can also stand for combat, pride, courage, and ferocity. Eagles traditionally were associated with nobility. They also can symbolize a father figure or the sun.

Ears To dream of human ears can be a warning to watch out what you say. Ears can also call attention to the need to listen carefully to what's going on around you.

Earthquake Dreaming of an earthquake might suggest that personal, financial, or business matters are unstable. Is there something upsetting taking place in your life?

Earthquakes can also have sexual connotations, such as the desire for sexual release. If there are others in the dream, does one of them make the "earth move" for you?

Eating A dream of eating might suggest a desire or craving for love or power. It can mean you are enjoying life or indulging in its pleasures. If you are the one being eaten in the dream, ask yourself if something is "eating at you." Do you feel as if you are being eaten alive?

Eclipse An eclipse suggests a disruption of the normal. When something is "eclipsed," it signifies a period of activity has ended. Also, an eclipse can mean that cosmic forces may be at work in your life.

Eel An eel can be a phallic symbol. Its movement through waters contains sexual overtones. Take your cues from what the eel is doing.

Egg In the Freudian interpretation, eggs can symbolize the male testicles and stand for virility. In the Jungian view, eggs represent wholeness, fertility, and new life. Eggs can also represent unhatched ideas; finding a nest of eggs might indicate a waiting period, or that ideas are gestating. What is the context of the dream? Is someone "egging" you on?

Elephant The appearance of these large, solid animals may portend the possession of wealth, honor, and a steadfast character. As the elephants rule in the wild, their appearance in your dream may suggest that you reign supreme in business and at home. How many elephants are you seeing? A herd of elephants may suggest great wealth, while a single elephant may represent a small but solid life.

Elevator Rising in an elevator may symbolize a raising of status, such as a promotion, or a raising of consciousness. Is the ascent rapid? Are you frightened? Exhilarated? A descent in an elevator might indicate a lowering in status or position, or a journey into the unconscious. Keep in mind that the dream might indicate hopes or fears rather than actual events. A stuck elevator might suggest that some aspect of your life is presently stuck. A plunging elevator could indicate a rapid descent into the unconscious.

Escaping If you dream of making an escape, consider whether you are avoiding something in your life, or whether you need to get away from something.

Evening A dream that takes place in the evening suggests uncertain or unrealized hopes. To dream of stars shining suggests present troubles followed by brighter times. A dream of lovers walking in the evening symbolizes separation.

Evergreen A dream of an evergreen—especially the word itself—might suggest a metaphor. To be "evergreen" indicates wealth or at least financial stability. An evergreen or pine tree might also indicate hope or even immortality. A decorated evergreen or Christmas tree suggests giving or receiving gifts.

Examination If you dream of taking an exam, it might indicate a concern about failure. A stack of tests could suggest you feel you are being tested too often. Look at the surrounding elements in the dream. If you forgot to go to class, the dream suggests that you are worried about being unprepared.

Explosion A dream of an explosion could be an attempt by your unconscious to get your attention to a matter of concern. An explosion could suggest a release or an outburst of repressed anger, or an upheaval in your life.

F

Falling Falling is a common dream symbol and usually an expression of a concern about failure. The dream could be a metaphor for falling down on the job. In most falling dreams, the dreamer never lands. If you do hit the ground, it could mean that you've struck bottom in a matter. If you get up unhurt, the dream may be suggesting that you won't be hurt by something that you perceive as a failure.

Fat A dream of being fat might be a concern about your diet, but it could also be a metaphor for wealth and abundance, or overindulging.

Father The appearance of your father can have many connotations, depending on the context of the dream and your relationship with him. Typically it represents a need for advice over a troubling situation.

EXERCISE 5: MY RECURRING DREAMS

Categorize three of your recurring dreams under broad topic headings like the ones presented in this chapter. Then, just as you did in Exercise 4, define what these symbols mean to you in your waking life. Do the definitions fit the dreams?

If these are recent dreams and you've recorded them in your journal, read them over and note what was going on in your life at the time you had the dreams. Then interpret the dreams.

Broad categories and meanings: _____

_____

_____

_____

What was going on in my life at the time of these dreams?

Dream 1 _____

_____

Dream 2 _____

_____

Dream 3 _____

_____

EXERCISE 5: MY RECURRING DREAMS

Interpretation of dreams:

Dream 1 _____
_____
_____

Dream 2 _____
_____
_____

Dream 3 _____
_____
_____

Notes _____
_____
_____
_____
_____
_____
_____

Father-in-Law To dream of your father-in-law suggests strife with friends or a family member. To see him happy and well augers pleasant family relations.

Feather To dream of a feather floating through the air bodes well. Your burdens will be light and easily borne. To dream of an eagle feather implies that your aspirations will be met.

February A dream of this short, winter month suggests continued ill health and melancholy. To dream of a sunshiny day in this month may suggest an unexpected change in fortune and outlook.

Fence A dream of a fence can indicate that you feel "fenced in." A fence can block you or it can protect you. If you are "on the

Family

To dream of members of your extended family is not always portentous. To dream of a cousin indicates you might have disappointment and sadness. Even dreaming of a friendly correspondence with your cousin signifies that there might be a major falling-out in the family.

If a woman dreams of her aunt, she will soon receive severe criticism of choices and actions she makes in life. And if a man or woman dreams of an uncle, beware, sad news will soon reach you.

Best not to dream about your extended family. Send them a card instead!

fence," the dream might suggest that you are undecided about something.

Fever To dream that you are suffering from a fever suggests a needless worry over a small affair.

Fight To fight in a dream may represent a conflict or the need to resolve an issue. Pay attention to other details in the dream in order to interpret it. Are you winning or losing a fight? Are you fighting with a loved one?

Fire Fire is generally a favorable symbol to the dreamer, as long as he or she is not burned, representing continued prosperity and fortune. If you're on fire, it's probably a metaphor for passion; it's as if you are burning with desire. Alternately, fire can symbolize destruction, a purification, illumination, and a spiritual awakening. Look at other metaphors: What are you getting "fired up"

about? Are you (or another figure in the dream) concerned about "being fired" or "getting burned"?

Fire Engine A symbol of distress and ultimately of protection, to dream of a fire engine indicates worry over an important matter at hand that will soon be resolved.

Fire Fighting To dream of fighting flames suggests that hard work is required before success in a matter at hand is achieved. To dream of a fire fighter may suggest solid friendships. To dream of an injured fire fighter indicates that a close friend may be in danger.

Fireworks A dream of fireworks suggests a celebration, a joyous explosion, or a release of repressed feelings.

Fish Fish swimming symbolize exploration of the unconscious or that which lies
below the surface. In the Freudian interpretation, fish are phallic symbols and
dreaming of fish is related to
sexual desires. The Jungian
interpretation is that fish
symbolize a spiritual quest
or seeking.

Flood A dream of a flood might suggest
that you are being overwhelmed by a rising
awareness of the unconscious aspects of
your being. A dream of flooding can also
serve as a warning that personal matters are
spilling over into other areas of your life.
Alternately, a flood can relate to a release of
sexual desires or a need to do so.

Flower Flowers in a dream can symbolize love and beauty. Flowers can also be a

symbol of the inner self. New blossoms suggest the opening of the inner self. Withered and dead flowers can mean disappointment and dismal situations.

Flying A flying dream may suggest the dreamer is soaring, or "flying high" as a result of a successful venture. Flying can also symbolize breaking free of restrictions or inhibitions. But flying itself can be a joyous experience in a dream no matter what the symbolic meaning.

Fog Dreaming of foggy conditions indicates a lack of clarity in some aspect of your life. Fog can also symbolize something hidden or something you're not seeing. Keep in mind that fog is usually short-lived and when it lifts, you will gain a new sense of clarity.

Flowers

To dream of a wreath of fresh flowers denotes that great opportunity will come your way. You'll have great success if you chose to take advantage of that opportunity.

But if you dream of a bier, which are the flowers on a coffin, no matter how fresh and beautiful the flowers are, you will know losses.

Happier circumstances are denoted by dreaming of bouquets, especially if they are made up of richly colored flowers. A legacy from an unknown and wealthy relative will soon be yours.

In addition there will probably be a pleasant gathering of young folks in your life.

Forest A forest suggests an exploration of the unconscious. It also can symbolize a need or desire to retreat from everyday life, to restore and revitalize your energies. To dream of a lush forest in complete foliage may mean prosperity and pleasure, whereas finding yourself in a dense forest may signify unpleasantness at home. A forest fire may symbolize the successful completion of your plans, with wealth and prosperity to follow.

Fountain A dream of a fountain can suggest longevity and virility. Water is related to the emotions and unconscious, so a fountain can indicate an emotional surge. Alternately, a dream of a fountain can indicate an examination of your emotions. What is the condition of the fountain? A clear fountain suggests vast possessions and many pleasures. A dry and broken fountain symbolizes the end of pleasure. A sparkling fountain in the moonlight can indicate an ill-advised pleasure.

Frog Frogs, like the prince who was turned into one, are transformative creatures. They start as tadpoles, grow legs and arms, and develop lungs. To dream of a frog may imply a major change or transformation in your life. Since frogs live part of their lives in water, a frog may also symbolize a leap into the unconscious.

Frost Frost, like ice, may represent an emotional state of the dreamer or a person in the dream. To see a friend or lover in frost could mean chilly feelings regarding the relationship.

G

Gambling Dreaming of gambling suggests taking a chance. If you are winning, it may bode well for a risky business deal. If you're watching others win, the game may symbolize a fear of taking a chance. Whether you should be more daring or play it safe depends on other factors in the dream.

Garbage To dream of garbage suggests a need to get rid of old, worn out ideas, or excess baggage in your life. Ask yourself if you are clinging to something or some condition that you no longer need?

Garden A garden sometimes indicates a need to bring more beauty into your life. It may be a metaphor for personal or spiritual growth, or a desire to cultivate a new talent or move into a higher realm of awareness. A garden with lots of weeds may symbolize a need to weed out old, outmoded ideas or a desire to cultivate your spiritual self.

Gate A gate may represent a portal from one state of being to another. Is there a gate-keeper? Do you meet the gatekeeper's criteria for passage to the next level? (see Door.)

Ghost An apparition or ghost appearing in a dream may suggest that something in your life is elusive or out of reach. If a person who has died appears in a dream, consider your past relationship to that person and what that individual symbolized in your life. A ghost of a living relative or friend in a dream may symbolize that you are in danger from someone you know, or if that ghost appears haggard it may symbolize an early death or a breaking off of a friendship.

Glass Glass is suggestive of separation and passive observation. Looking through glass in a dream may symbolize bitter disappointment clouding your brightest hopes. Receiving cut glass in a dream may suggest a reward for your efforts.

Gold Dreaming of gold jewelry or coins or a gold object indicates that success is forthcoming.

Goose A goose is often associated with a golden egg so that dreaming of one is a symbol of abundance. On the other hand, a goose in the oven or on fire suggests "your

goose is cooked." Alternately, a "big goose egg" can mean zero or nothing.

Grave Like many dream symbols, a grave is one that grabs your attention, especially if it's your grave. A grave may portend a death, but not necessarily a physical one. It may mean that you're leaving the old behind, moving on to something new. As a metaphor, a grave suggests that you may be dealing with a grave matter.

Green When green is a dominant color in a dream, it can be interpreted symbolically, like any object in a dream. Green is a color of healing, of growth, of money, and of new beginnings. It suggests positive movement in a matter at hand.

Gun A gun in your possession can symbolize protection, but it is also a phallic

Grass, Pasture, Fields

To dream of green fields, ripe with corn or grain, indicates you will have great abundance. If you dream of plowed fields, you will have wealth and prestige at a young age. Of course if you dream of a field full of dead corn, expect a dreary future.

If you dream of a pasture freshly plowed and ready for planting, a long struggle will soon be resolved and you will have great success.

To dream of green grass signifies good things will happen in your life. If you are in business, you will soon be wealthy. If you are an artist, you soon will become well-known. If you are about to marry, you will have a safe, happy life with your partner.

symbol and a sign of aggressive male behavior. If you shoot yourself, the act is what's important, not the gun.

H

Hail To dream of being in a hailstorm, or to hear hail knocking against the house represents being besieged by a troubling matter, thoughts, or emotions. However, if you dream of watching hail fall through sunshine and rain, it may suggest that fortune and pleasure will shine on you after a brief period of trouble or misery.

Hair Hair can appear in many different ways and is open to many interpretations. To dream that you have a beautiful head of hair and are combing it indicates thoughts of appearance over substance. To see your hair turn unexpectedly white suggests sudden misfortune and grief over a situation at hand, while a dream that you have a full head of white hair suggests a pleasing and fortunate passage through life. For a man to dream that his hair is thinning suggests misfortune due to generosity, or illness through worry. To see yourself covered in hair represents an indulgence in vice, while a dream of tangled and unkempt hair suggests trouble or concern over a matter at hand. For a woman to compare a white hair with a black one taken from her head symbolizes a hesitation between two paths.

Hammer A hammer may suggest strength or power. However, because it can be used for either constructive or destructive purposes, how the hammer is used is the key to its meaning.

Hand A dream of a hand (or hands) is open to numerous interpretations, depending on what the hand (or hands) is doing and the surrounding circumstances. Shaking hands is an act of friendship or an agreement. Hands folded in prayer may suggest you are seeking help or pursuing religious or spiritual urgings. A hand that is grasping at something may suggest a fear of death. As a metaphor, a hand may suggest that something important is "at hand." To see beautiful hands in a dream signifies feelings of great honor and rapid advancement in a matter at hand. Ugly and malformed hands point to disappointment and poverty. A detached hand represents solitude; people may fail to understand your views and feeling in a matter. Burning your hands in a dream suggests that you have overreached your abilities and will suffer some loss because of it. A dream of washing your hands indicates participation in some joyous affair.

Harvest A harvest represents completion and abundance, and may indicate that your reward is due. As with all symbols, personal connotations are important. For instance, if you grew up on a farm, the dream could mean a longing to return to the past or to simpler times.

Hat A hat covers the head and can suggest that the person wearing it is concealing something, as in "keep it under your hat." Dreaming that you have a feather in your hat indicates achievement.

Hawk A hawk is a creature with keen sight. A soaring hawk in a dream might suggest the need for insight. It also might mean that the dreamer should keep a "hawk's eye" on someone or a situation.

Head Dreaming of a human head could indicate that you are ahead, or successful, on a matter of importance. A head also symbolizes a source of wisdom.

Heart To see a heart might relate to romantic inclinations. Is there a "heart throb" in your life? Alternately, the image might suggest you get to the "heart of the matter." On the negative side, if your heart is bleeding, it may mean that excessive sympathy is becoming a burden for you or the recipient, or both.

Heel The heel of your foot or shoe may symbolize vulnerability, as in the Achilles' heel story. It might also stand for an oppressive situation, as in "under someone's heel." Are you dealing with someone who is not trustworthy? He or she could be the heel in question.

Helmet Wearing a helmet in a dream denotes protection. The helmet could also symbolize that you need to guard your time, thoughts, or ideas.

High Tide To dream of a high tide symbolizes that a change, usually favorable, is in order, as in the phrase the "tides are turning."

Hogs A fat hog in a dream may suggest abundance, while a lean, hungry hog may foretell a troubling situation. If you grew up on a farm with hogs, the dream could relate to some aspect of your childhood. If the hogs are wallowing in mud, the indication might be that you've lowered your standards regarding a matter, or that you are groveling. The dream could also be a warning of such possibilities. A squealing hog suggests that something distasteful has occurred or will soon occur.

Horse A horse symbolizes strength, power, endurance, majesty, and virility. A man dreaming of a horse might desire virility and sexual prowess; a woman might be expressing a desire for sexual intercourse. Riding a horse suggests one is in a powerful position. White horses represent purity, while black horses represent a postponement of pleasure.

Hospital Finding oneself in a hospital suggests a need for healing, or a concern about one's health. Seeing someone else in a hospital might indicate that person is in a weakened condition. If you work in a hospital, the meaning of the dream may relate to work matters. In the latter case, other circumstances in the dream should be examined.

House Houses are common forums for dreams and may be of little consequence unless the house itself is the focus of the dream. If so, examine the type of house and its size. Discovering new rooms in a house or following secret passages in an old house can relate to an exploration of the unconscious. A small house might suggest a feeling of confinement. If a house is under construction, it could symbolize growth. If it's dilapidated, it suggests improvements are needed in some part of the dreamer's life.

Hugging To dream of your hugging a stranger suggests that you crave affection. If you know the person you are hugging, the interpretation will depend on your relationship to that person.

Humidity Dreaming of humidity represents the presence of an oppressive situation, either in work or at home.

Hurricane Destructive and unpredictable, hurricane dreams can suggest different meanings depending on their context in the dream. To hear and see a hurricane coming

at you symbolizes a feeling of torture and sus-
pense over a matter at hand in which you are
trying to avert failure. To dream of looking at
the debris of a hurricane suggests that you will
come close to calamity, but will be saved by
the efforts of others. A dream in which you are
in a house that is shattered by a hurricane and
you are trying to save someone caught in the
rubble may represent that your life will suffer
many changes but that there is still no peace in
domestic or business matters. To see people
dead and wounded suggests that you are concerned over the troubles of others.

Ice Ice may symbolize an emotional state
of the dreamer or a person in the dream. Are
you receiving an "icy reception?" If you are in
a tenuous situation, you could be "skating on
thin ice." In a sexual context, ice is frigidity.

To dream of ice floating in a clear stream signifies an interruption of happiness, while dreaming of eating ice portends sickness.

Ice cream A dream of ice cream, especially melting ice cream, may suggest that obstacles are being removed and that there is reason to celebrate. If ice cream is your favorite dessert, then the dream suggests that you're being rewarded or have reason to treat yourself. It can also stand for a desire for sexual fulfillment.

Icicles Icicles represent danger or your concern over a matter that is hanging over you in some way. To dream of icicles falling off of trees or the eaves of a house may suggest that some misfortune will soon disappear. To dream of icicles on evergreens symbolizes that a bright future may be overshadowed by doubt.

Illness If you dream of being ill, ask yourself if you're in need of being cared for and pampered. This dream might also be a message to watch your health.

Incest A dream of a sexual encounter with someone within your family is not necessarily a warning about incest. Examine your relationship with the person in question. If there have been arguments or you're alienated from this family member, the dream may be your inner self expressing your love in a shocking way that will catch your attention.

Infants Seeing infants in a dream suggests that pleasant surprises are near. Seeing an infant swimming represents a fortunate escape from some endeavor.

Initiation Initiation suggests that a new path is opening for you. It could be a career change or advancement. Often, initiatory dreams relate to a spiritual quest.

Insects What's annoying or "bugging you"? If you dream of ants, you may be feeling "antsy" about a matter. (see Ant.)

Interview Being interviewed in a dream is similar to taking an examination. It suggests you're being judged. If you're surprised by the interview, it may indicate that you are feeling unprepared.

Invalid A dream of an invalid may indicate that you (or someone else) feel weak or incapable of living independently.

Island An island can be viewed as an exotic place or as a separate, isolated land. Dreaming of an island might mean that a

Ivy & Mistletoe

Dreaming of ivy growing on trees or a house indicates you will have excellent health and success. Many joys in your life could follow this dream. For a young woman to dream of ivy clinging to a wall in moonlight portends she will have a secret affair with a young man. Beware of dreaming of withered ivy. It indicates broken engagements and sadness.

To dream of mistletoe signifies great happiness and honor is to come your way. If you are young and dream of mistletoe, it indicates you will have many pleasant times in your future.

vacation is due, especially if "going to the islands" is a vacation destination. Alternately, finding yourself on an "desert island" may suggest you are cut off from others or from your inner self.

J

Jail A jail may indicate that you're feeling restricted or confined and fear being punished. Or you may believe that you should be punished. Dreaming of being a jailer suggests the desire to control others or to gain more control of your own life.

January To dream of this month may mean that you will be associated with unloved companions or children.

Jaws Do you feel like you're under attack? Jaws can be the entry point to an archetypal journey into the underworld. Such a dream might also relate to a disagreement.

Jewelry In a material sense, jewelry can symbolize affluence, but look to other aspects of the dream for confirmation. Jewelry can also stand for inner wealth, psychic protection, or healing.

Job Dreaming that you are at work on the job may indicate that you're overworked, you're deeply focused on some aspect of your job, or you desire to work harder and achieve more.

Judge If you're the judge, the dream suggests that you have a choice to make. A judge can also represent justice or fairness. Alternately, a judge may stand for a part of you that criticizes your impulsive behavior. Or perhaps you're concerned that you're being judged. Who is judging you?

July A dream that takes place in this month symbolizes a depressed outlook that will suddenly change to unimagined pleasure and good fortune.

Jumping Pick your metaphor: Are you "a jump ahead," "jumping to conclusions," "jumping the gun," or "jumping for joy"? A series of jumps may be the take-off point for a flying dream. A great leap can also symbolize success or achievement or "a leap of faith."

June For a dream to take place in June symbolizes unusual gains in all undertakings. For a woman to dream of vegetation, dying, or a drought suggests a lasting sorrow and loss.

Jungle A jungle may represent a hidden, dark part of the self that you've been avoiding.

Your unconscious might be telling you of a need to explore this part of yourself. It may also represent a great, untapped fertility within you for spiritual growth.

Junk If you dream of junk or clutter, ask yourself if you're clinging to the past, to things or ideas that are no longer useful. If something you value appears as junk in a dream, it may indicate that you need to reassess your values.

K

Kangaroo To see a kangaroo might suggest the dreamer is "hopping mad" about something. It could also mean that you have the ability to "hop to" a particular matter that is pending.

Key A key can stand for a part of yourself that you've locked away, or something that you can now access if you have the key. Such a dream may also indicate you hold the key to your own concerns.

Killing A dream of killing someone is probably not a warning that you might turn into a killer. Instead, the meaning is more likely a symbolic act of aggression. Who did you kill and how is that person involved in your life? If you don't recognize the person, the dream may symbolize killing off an unwanted part of yourself.

King A king is a ruler and a powerful authority figure. Dreaming of a king may mean you are seeking status or support. The king may represent your father or some other powerful figure in your life. If you're the king, the indication is that you have achieved a high level of authority or are a highly capable individual.

Kiss A kiss suggests a romantic involvement, but can also be a metaphor as in "kiss and make up," or the "kiss of death." In the former, the dream kiss might indicate a reconciliation is as hand. A kiss of death spells the end to something, such as a way of life. For married people to kiss each other symbolizes harmony in the home life. Is it dark or light out during the kiss? The former suggests danger or an illicit situation while the latter represents honorable intentions. To dream of kissing someone on the neck symbolizes a passionate inclination in a matter at hand.

Kitchen Going to a kitchen in a dream suggests some part of your life is in need of nourishment. Alternately, a kitchen might suggest that something is in the process of being "cooked up," like a new project. Note what you're doing in the kitchen.

Kitten To discover kittens in a closet or a basement suggests the awakening of hidden aspects of the self. It can also relate to new ideas and projects.

Knife A knife is a symbol of aggression and the male sexual organ. Examine the other aspects of the dream. Are you being stabbed in the back? Do you hold the knife or is someone threatening you with it? A rusty knife may symbolize dissatisfaction, a sharp knife worry, and a broken knife defeat.

Knight A knight signifies honor and high standing. Are you searching for a knight or are you acting like a knight? Knights are also armored and stand for protection.

Knob A knob appearing in a dream may imply a need to get a handle on a matter. Knobs also signify a means of passing from one room to the next, or one way of life to another.

Knot Dreaming of knots suggests that you're all tied up about something—that worries and anxieties are troubling you. You may feel as if you're "tied in a knot." Alternately, if you or someone close to you is "tying the knot," the dream might signify a concern about an upcoming marriage.

Friendship–Neighbors

If you dream of a gathering of your friends and they are all happy, you will have a pleasant event to attend soon. If you dream of a gathering of your friends and they are sad and gloomy—call them; something is probably amiss.

If you dream of a neighbor, be prepared to spend hours ironing out problems due to unwarranted gossip. If you dream your neighbor is sad—watch out. You might quarrel with that neighbor.

L

Laboratory A laboratory is a place where experiments are conducted. The implication is that the dreamer is unsatisfied with a present situation and experimenting with something new. The dreamer might also be testing a relationship with someone.

Labyrinth A dream of a labyrinth may indicate that you feel trapped in a situation or a relationship and are looking for a way out. It may also refer to the intricacies of a spiritual journey.

Ladder Are you going up or climbing down the ladder? An ascent may symbolize a higher step into an inner realm or a promotion to a higher status in one's career or other pursuits.

Lagoon Lagoons symbolize doubt and confusion over an emotional matter or a stagnant situation.

Lake In the Freudian interpretation, a lake is symbolic of the vagina. In the Jungian world, lakes and other bodies of water stand for the unconscious or emotions. In one interpretation, the dreamer who dives into a lake is returning to the womb. In the other, the dreamer explores the unconscious. But if neither interpretation fits, examine the other elements in the dream. Is the lake clear or muddy? The former suggests lucidity and strength of purpose, while the latter may represent muddled feelings and an unsure direction in a matter at hand.

Lamb A lamb may stand for gentleness or vulnerability, as in "a lamb to the slaughter," or it may be a spiritual symbol as in "sacrificial lamb" and "lamb of God." However, a dream of a lamb may simply symbolize a general love of animals.

Lamp A lamp, like a lantern, represents light or illumination and suggests the dreamer is searching for truth.

Lap A symbol of security, such as "the lap of luxury," to dream of sitting on someone's lap signifies safety from some troubling situation. A dream of a cat in a lap represents danger from a seductive enemy.

Law suits Dreams of legal matters suggest the dreamer is being judged.

Leeches Leeches are nightmarish creatures that suck blood. Is there someone in your life who is draining you of energy?

Legs Legs in various states of health and appearance are frequently seen in dreams and open to many interpretations depending on the context. To dream of admiring well-shaped legs suggests a loss of judgment; to see misshapen legs represents unsuccessful endeavors and ill-tempered friends. A wooden leg represents deception to friends, while a wounded leg suggests a loss of power and standing. A dream of ulcers on your legs suggests a drain on your resources to help others. A young woman who admires her own legs indicates vanity, and if she has hairy legs then it may indicate feelings of domination over her mate. Dreaming that your own legs are clean and well shaped represents a happy future with faithful friends.

Letter A letter sometimes symbolizes a message from your unconscious to you. If you're unable to read the letter, look at other aspects of the dream for clues. An anonymous letter may signify an injurious concern from an unspecified source. Blue ink symbolizes steadfastness and affection, red ink may suggest suspicion and jealousy, and a letter with a black border may represent distress and death of some kind. Receiving a letter written on black paper with white ink may suggest feelings of misery and disappointment over a matter. If this letter passed between husband and wife or lovers, then concerns over the relationship may be present. A torn letter may suggest concerns that hopeless mistakes may ruin your reputation.

Lightning A dream of lightning indicates a flash of inspiration or sudden awareness about the truth of a matter. Lightning can also mean a purging or purification, or fear of authority or death.

Lion To dream of a lion signifies that you are driven by a great force. Subduing a lion indicates victory in a matter. If you are over-taken by the lion, the dream suggests that you may be vulnerable to an attack of some sort. A caged lion may mean that you will succeed as long as the opposition is held in check.

Lottery To dream of a lottery signifies chance or throwing your fate to luck. If you dream of holding the winning number, then luck and good fortune in a matter at hand may follow. To see others winning in a lottery may suggest that many friends will be brought together in a pleasing manner. A young

Leopards, Zebras

Dreaming of zebras running fast on the hoof indicates you are interested in fleeting enterprises. If you dream of a zebra wild in its native environment, you might pursue a fancy that could bring unsatisfactory results. Beware of those with multi-colored stripes!

If you dream of a leopard attacking you, your future success may encounter many difficulties. But if you kill the leopard, you will be victorious in life. If you dream of a caged leopard, it means that although your enemies surround you, they will fail to injure you.

woman dreaming of a lottery may indicate a reckless attitude.

Luggage Luggage stands for your personal effects or what you carry with you on a journey. What happens to the luggage? Lost luggage might be a concern about your identity or about being prepared for the journey. Stolen luggage might suggest that you feel someone is interfering with your attempt to reach a goal.

Magic This could point to the magical aspects of creativity or, on the darker side, to deceit and trickery.

Man To dream of a handsome man, some individual you do not know, represents an enjoyment of life. If the man is disfigured, then perplexities and sorrow may involve you in a matter at hand. For a woman to dream of a handsome man can suggest that distinction will be offered.

Manuscript A manuscript represents the collection of your hopes and desires. To interpret the dream, note the shape or appearance of the manuscript. Is it finished or unfinished? Are you at work on it? Did you lose it?

Map You're searching for a new path to follow or are being guided in a new direction.

March A dream that occurs in this month may symbolize unsatisfactory results in a business matter.

Mask Masks hide our appearances and our feelings from others, but the dream may signify that you are hiding your emotions on a particular matter from yourself. If others are wearing masks, then perhaps you are confronted with a situation in which you think someone is not being truthful.

May A dream of May indicates fortunate times and pleasures for the young. To dream of a freakish appearance of nature suggests sudden sorrow and misery.

Medicine Taking medicine in a dream can be a potent symbol of healing your "wounds." It also suggests that you have "to take your medicine," do what is necessary or required of you.

Merry-go-round A merry-go-round suggests that you are going round and round in life and not moving ahead. The same would apply to someone else you dream of on a merry-go-round.

Meteor A meteor or falling star may symbolize that your wish will come true, or it could suggest that you are engaged in wishful thinking. Look at the other elements in the dream and decide which possibility is true for you.

Microphone A microphone may symbolize the desire to draw attention to yourself, or to gain power over others. Alternately, a microphone may suggest a concern that you are not forceful enough, and need help in projecting yourself.

Microscope A microscope symbolizes the need or wish to find something that's out of sight or hidden from you.

Milk Milk symbolizes nurturing. It can also represent strength and virility.

Mist Like fog, mist indicates a period of temporary uncertainty. Seeing others in a mist may mean that you will profit by their misfortune and uncertainty.

Money Money represents energy, power, and influence. Dreaming of gaining money suggests abundance; losing sums of money symbolizes a draining of energy, power, and influence. To dream of stealing money suggests danger.

Morning Morning represents a fresh start, or a sudden change of fortune for the positive. To dream of a cloudy morning indicates that heavy matters may overwhelm you.

Mother To see your mother symbolizes pleasing results from any endeavor. What is the context in which she appears? To converse with her suggests you may soon receive good news. To hear your mother calling represents that you are in need of a correction in your life.

Mother-in-Law A dream in which your mother-in-law appears suggests that a pleasant reconciliation is in order over a matter after some serious disagreement.

Mountain A mountain represents a challenge. If you're climbing the mountain, you're working to achieve your goals. Descending a mountain suggests that things are easier now; your success may have ensured your future.

Mule Mules are known for their contrary behavior, as in "stubborn as a mule." To dream of a mule suggests that the dreamer may be acting in a stubborn manner that others find annoying. Mules also are work animals. Consider whether you are rebelling against some aspect of your job or career.

Murder Murder symbolizes repressed anger either at yourself or others. If you murder someone you know, consider your relationship with that person. If you're the one murdered, then the dream may symbolize a personal transformation.

Music Music in a dream symbolizes emotional matters. Consider the type of music you heard and how you related to it. Did it fill you with joy? Did it make you sad or angry?

N

Nail A nail in a dream can have a variety of meanings. To "nail it down" suggests putting something together or holding it together

Naked/Nudity Being nude in a dream can symbolize a wish for exposure, to be seen or heard. It can also relate to a need to bare the truth. Alternately, a dream of nudity can be sexually related and suggests that the dreamer is no longer inhibited. To dream of swimming naked may represent an illicit affair that will end badly, or that you have many admirers.

Neck A neck can be a sexual symbol related to the slang term necking. A neck can also represent taking a chance, as in "sticking one's neck out." Alternately, if there is pain related to this part of the body, something might be giving you a "pain in the neck."

Needle A dream of a needle and thread might indicate that a matter is being sewn up, or a deal is being completed. A needle might also suggest that someone is needling you. To dream of threading a needle symbolizes that you may be burdened with caring for others, to look for a needle augers useless worries. To break a needle in a dream signifies loneliness and poverty.

Nest A nest is a symbol of home and might relate to the desire to return home. If you are moving, it might relate to your concerns about your new home. If there is an egg in the nest, the dream might relate to a concern about your savings or "nest egg."

Night A night setting for a dream might suggest something is hidden or obscured. There might be a need to illuminate something. Being surrounded by night in a dream suggests oppression and hardship.

Nose A nose can be a symbol of intrusive behavior, as in "sticking one's nose into someone else's business." Dreaming of a nose may suggest that someone is interfering in your life or that you are being nosy.

November November dreams usually suggest a season of indifferent success in all affairs.

Nurse A dream of a nurse suggests that you are being healed or are in need of healing. It also implies a desire to be pampered or nursed. The dream could also relate to a relationship or a project that you are nursing along.

Nursing A dream of nursing could indicate an idea or situation that needs nurturing.

Oak An oak tree represents strength, stability, endurance, truth, and wisdom. A dream with an oak may suggest that a strong, proper foundation has been established in a matter.

Oar An oar can represent masculinity and strength; it dips into the water, the emotions. To row vigorously suggests a need for aggressiveness or that you are moving through an issue. If you have only one oar and are rowing in a circle, it might suggest frustration at the lack of forward movement.

Oasis An oasis suggests that you've arrived at a place of sustenance, that you are being nurtured. Or it might suggest that you're taking a break from your journey or have succeeded in reaching one destination on the journey. Alternately, the dream might imply that you need a vacation, a break.

Ocean A dream of the ocean often represents the emotional setting of your life. The context of the dream is important here. Sailing through rough seas suggests you are capable of dealing with life's ups and downs. Large waves can also represent untapped powers of the unconscious. Fishing in the ocean and catching something big can suggest an opportunity is at hand or that you are delving into the wealth of your unconscious. To be lost at sea may suggest you have lost your moorings, that you are adrift in life and in need of direction. To be anchored in the ocean may indicate you have found a place in life.

October To dream of October portends success. New friendships or business affairs will ripen into lasting relationships.

Officer An officer, whether military, police, or corporate, represents an authority figure. Dreaming of an officer, especially if you don't know the person, can suggest a fear or wariness of authority figures or a need for guidance from a person with authority.

Oil A dream of oil represents great wealth or inner wealth, as in a dream of pumping crude oil to the surface. Using aromatic oils in a dream can represent sacred matters. A person associated with oil might be slick, or a smooth-talker.

Old man If the old man guides or directs you in some way, he is, in Jungian thought, an archetypal figure. If the man appears to be weak or injured in some way, he could symbolize some part of yourself that needs attention or someone in your life who needs your help. It may also mean that you need to redefine your beliefs about aging.

Old woman In Jungian terms, an old woman is an archetypal symbol of the power of the feminine, or the gatekeeper between life and death. If she is weak or injured, she may represent a part of yourself that needs attention or someone in your life who needs your help.

Oven An oven might represent a gestation period. It also symbolizes the womb and feminine energy. A dream of an oven could relate to a pregnancy.

Owl An owl represents both wisdom and mystery and is a symbol of the unconscious.

Ox To dream of an ox implies great strength and endurance and an ability to carry on against great odds.

P

Painting If a wall is being painted, the act may suggest that something is being hidden or covered up. Painting at an easel may indicate artistic or creative talents are ready to be expressed.

Park Dreaming of a park may suggest a wish to relax and enjoy life. Walking in an unlit park at night may mean that you are delving into areas of darkness and danger, or that you are dealing with hidden or mysterious matters.

Party To find yourself at a party in a dream suggests that a celebration is in order. If you are concerned about a particular matter that remains unsettled, the dream may indicate a favorable resolution.

Peacock A dream of a peacock suggests that you have something to show off, a reason to be proud, similar to the peacock that displays its colorful tail feathers.

Photograph Since a photograph is an image of a person or object rather than the real thing, a dream of a photograph hints of deception. If you recognize a person in a dream photo, be careful in your dealings with the person and look for hidden meaning in the person's actions. To dream of having your own photograph made suggests that you may unwittingly be the cause of your own troubles.

Physician A physician appearing in a dream might indicate that a healing is at hand. A physician is also an authority figure who might be offering a diagnosis on some matter. Sometimes, a physician may take the form of a trusted friend who isn't a doctor but whose nurturing traits are healing.

Piano Music in general represents joyous or festive feelings. Note the condition and type of music coming from the piano. A broken piano symbolizes displeasure in your achievements; an old-fashioned piano suggests neglect over a matter at hand.

Pill Taking a pill in a dream suggests that the dreamer may be required to go along with something unpleasant. But positive results should follow.

Pilot A pilot symbolizes someone soaring high and in control in spite of the fast pace. A dream of a pilot may represent that you're in the pilot's seat concerning some issue in your life.

Planet Seeing a planet or visiting another planet in a dream may indicate a new adventure, a new way of thinking, or a new dimension of creativity.

Polar Bear These creatures may represent that trickery or deceit is upon you. Maybe one of your enemies will appear as a friend to overcome you. However, seeing the skin of a polar bear suggests that you will successfully triumph over adversity.

Police Police officers represent authority; they uphold the law. A dream of police may serve as a warning against breaking the law or bending rules. It might suggest a fear of punishment. Alternately, the dream may indicate a desire for justice and to punish the wrong-doers in a matter of concern.

Pond A pond signifies tranquility and a placid outlook in either the dreamer or a person in the dream.

Pregnant If a woman dreams of being pregnant, it could indicate a desire for a child or the onset of the condition. A pregnancy could also symbolize something new coming into being in the dreamer's life, an idea or project that is gestating.

Priest A priest represents a benign spiritual authority who serves as a guide. Alternately, a priest might symbolize a dictatorial figure or one who judges and condemns. A dream of a priest may indicate the need to follow or eschew conventional religion. Look to surrounding details for clarification.

Prison Constraint and restriction are implied. If you see yourself at work in a prison, the dream might suggest that you've limited your creativity or that you feel it's difficult to "escape" your job for a better one.

Professor A professor may represent knowledge, wisdom, and higher education.

Prophet A prophet provides knowledge, guidance, and perhaps a peek at the future. Or, the symbol may indicate that you're in need of guidance.

Puddle Stepping into or stomping through puddles represents a parting or clearing away of troubles, with good times to follow. To dream that you are just wetting your feet in a puddle may mean that trouble will follow a pleasurable experience.

Pump To see a pump in a dream denotes that energy is available to meet your needs. A functioning pump could also symbolize good health. A broken pump signifies a breakdown or disruption of the usual way of doing things.

Puppet A dream of a puppet might indicate that you are feeling manipulated in some aspect of your life. Alternately, if you are behind the puppet, the dream may indicate that you're acting in a manipulative manner.

Q

Quarrel A dream of a quarrel may indicate that an inner turmoil is plaguing you. If the person you're quarreling with is identifiable, look at your relationship with the person and see if you can identify the area of disagreement. There could be clues in the dream that indicate a way to resolve the differences.

Queen Both an authority and a mother figure, the queen is an archetypal symbol of power. If you are the queen, the dream may be suggesting a desire for leadership. If someone

else is the queen, the dream may indicate that you see the woman as capable and powerful.

Quest A dream of a quest may indicate a desire to achieve a goal or embark on an adventure.

Quicksand A dream of quicksand indicates that you need to watch where you are headed. If you're already in the quicksand, then you're probably mired in an emotional matter and feel as if you can't escape. It could refer to either business or personal matters.

Quilt A quilt suggests warmth and protection. A patchwork quilt symbolizes the sewing together of various aspects of your life to form a protective covering.

EXERCISE 6: BRAINSTORMING

This is a brainstorming session to find hidden talents and abilities you may have but haven't fully developed. Some of the questions you might ask yourself include the following:

☆ Are your hobbies and passions separate from your job or integrated into it?

☆ What kind of work would you like to do?

☆ What's holding you back from your heart's desire?

☆ How would you expand your present work/career?

☆ What is your "ideal" job or career?

Undeveloped talents and abilities _____

_____

_____

What I may want to work on: _____

_____

_____

(continued)

What I would like to be doing: _____

_____

_____

Steps I can take toward this goal: _____

_____

_____

What I hope to achieve: _____

_____

_____

Now describe at least three dreams you've had that deal with abilities and talents that are now dormant in your life, but which you would like to develop.

Talents of my future self

Dream 1

_____

_____

_____

_____

_____

_____

Dream 2

_____

_____

_____

_____

_____

Dream 3

_____

_____

_____

_____

_____

Ribbons, Tassels, Epaulets

—■—

If you should dream of ribbons floating from the costume of another person, you will have happy and pleasant friendships and everyday cares will not be troubling. To dream of buying ribbons denotes a happy life. Dreaming of decorating yourself with ribbons signifies you will soon have a good offer of marriage.

To dream of tassels means you will reach the top of your desires. But to dream of losing tassels means you might go through unpleasant experiences.

For a man to dream of epaulets means he might be in disfavor among his friends for a time. If a woman dreams of meeting a man wearing epaulets, beware, it denotes she is about to form an unwise alliance that might end in scandal.

R

Rabbit The rabbit is a symbol of fertility and magic, as the rabbit pulled from the magician's hat. Although fertility could relate to the conception of children, it might also concern financial abundance, the success of a particular project, or other matters. A white rabbit may signify faithfulness in love.

Race If you are racing in a dream, then perhaps you're involved in an overly competitive situation or you're in a rush. The message might be that it's time to slow down and relax.

Rain A fresh downpour symbolizes a washing or cleansing away of the old. Alternately, a rainy day may indicate a gloomy situation. To hear the patter of rain on the roof may signify domestic bliss, while seeing a downpour of rain from inside a house may represent requited love and fortune. Seeing it rain on others may mean that you are excluding friends from your confidence.

Rainbow Usually seen after rain storms in nature, their appearance in dreams may represent that favorable conditions will arise after a brief period of unpleasantness. Seeing a low-hanging rainbow over verdant trees may signify success in any endeavor.

Rams If you dream of a ram charging you with its head down, that indicates you are under attack from some quarter. If the ram is near, it may indicate that the attack is near or that you will have little time to react. A ram charging from a distance suggests that you will have time to respond to the situation. Consider whether someone in your life is trying to "ram" something down your throat. If the ram is quietly grazing in a pasture, the indication could be that you have powerful allies on your side.

Rapids Rapids represent danger and a fear of being swept away by emotions.

Rat Rats are generally associated with filth and dilapidation. Dreaming of a rat or rats may suggest the deterioration of a situation. Ask yourself who the "rat" is in your life.

Red The color red is often associated with vitality and energy, the heart, and blood. The color red in a dream can also mean anger or strong emotions as in "seeing red." Red often indicates that the dream originates from the deepest level of your being.

Referee A referee in a dream can symbolize an inner battle taking place or it can relate to conflict in your daily life. Can you identify the issue? If so, weigh the two sides, negotiate, and reach a settlement. Sometimes working with a third party, not involved in the dispute, can help.

Rice Rice is the dietary staple of the majority of the world's population. To dream of rice is a symbol of fertility and good fortune.

River A dream of floating down a river might indicate a lack of motivation. Are you allowing surrounding circumstances to direct

your life, rather than taking charge? A dream of a surging, frothing river may relate to deep-seated anger. In mythology, a river sometimes relates to death or the passing from one state to another.

Road A road is a means of getting from one place to another. What is the condition of the road in your dream? A smooth and straight road suggests the path ahead is easy. A road with dips and curves may indicate that you need to be aware, flexible, and ready for change. A roadblock suggests that there are detours in your path.

Rose A rose symbolizes the feminine and is associated with romance, beauty, and love. A dream of someone handing you a rose may indicate an offering of love. A rose can also relate to good and evil. If someone crushes a rose, that person's intent might be evil.

Ruins To dream of something in ruins suggests the deterioration of some condition in your life. Keep in mind that when things fall apart an opportunity to rebuild inevitably appears. If you are planning a trip, especially one to another culture, a dream of ancient ruins could symbolize the adventure of the journey ahead. Alternately, it could signify that you have the ability to access knowledge or wisdom from the past.

Running When you run in a dream, it might be either toward or away from something; you may be in a hurry to escape from something or to reach a goal. Depending on the circumstances, the dream may indicate that you need to hurry, or that you're rushing around too much and need to rest. Are you running alone or with others? The former may symbolize that you will overcome your competition in business matters, while the latter may represent your participation in a joyous occasion.

S

Sacrifice To see yourself sacrificed in a dream suggests that you're giving up something important for the sake of others. Closely examine your feelings about the matter. Decide what changes, if any, need to be made.

Sailor A dream of a sailor suggests that you are working on a ship. Symbolically, it could mean that you are working on matters dealing with the unconscious or emotions. (see Ship and Water.)

Saint A saint in a dream indicates you're being guided or are seeking guidance from a higher source.

School A school dream may indicate that you are gaining knowledge at a deep level of your existence or that what you are learning in your waking life is being processed and adapted by the unconscious. What happens in the school is important in the interpretation. If you're late to class or show up to take a test without ever having gone to class, the dream is a common symbol for feeling unprepared for something in your life. If you're looking for a school or classroom, the dream may be telling you that expanding your education is in order.

Scissors Is there something in your life you want to cut off? Scissors also indicate a need to "cut it out." The person with the scissors may be acting "snippy."

Scrapbook Scrapbooks are full of things from the past that are filed away and forgotten. Note the other details of the dream. Are you viewing a scrapbook with someone? What are you placing in the scrapbook? It may suggest that you have an unpleasant situation that needs to be put in the past.

Sea Dreams of the sea represent unfulfilled longings or unchanging emotions.

September Dreaming of September represents good luck and fortune.

Shadow Dreaming of your shadow may suggest that you need to address hidden parts of yourself. Perhaps you do not accept these darker aspects of your personality and project them onto others. The dream may also suggest that you need to incorporate the shadow side into your psyche.

Shaking Hands The handshake marks either a new beginning or an ending to a situation. Are you saying farewell to  someone in a dream? Then perhaps you are saying goodbye to a matter at hand. To dream of shaking hands with a prominent leader may mean you will be held in esteem by strangers in a new situation.

Shaving Is there something in your life that needs cleaning up or removed? To dream of shaving yourself connotes that you are in charge of your future. Shaving with a dull razor suggests a troublesome or painful issue. A clean shaven countenance suggests a smooth journey through a matter at hand.

Sheep Do you perceive yourself as one of a flock? This can be a comforting image in terms of being part of a community. Or it may indicate that you lack individuality or the will to strike out on your own.

Shell A shell usually symbolizes a womb. Depending on the circumstances of the dream, it can portend a birth of a child or a new project. A shell can also symbolize protection.

Ship Since a ship travels on water, the dream may signify a voyage through the unconscious or a journey involving your emotions. The state of the ship and the condition of the water should be considered in the interpretation. To see a ship in a storm may indicate your concern over a tempestuous or unfortunate affair, either in business or personal matters. To dream of others shipwrecked may symbolize a feeling of inadequacy in protecting friends or family.

Shoes Shoes are a means of moving ahead. Shiny, new shoes might suggest a journey is about to begin. Well-worn shoes, on the other hand, might indicate that one is weary of the journey or that it is near completion. Mismatched shoes might indicate that the journey is multifaceted. Consider the old cliche: "If the shoe fits, wear it."

Shovel A tool for digging, a shovel in a dream may indicate that you are searching for something or are about to embark on a quest for inner knowledge. A shovel might also represent labor or hard work ahead. A broken shovel could mean that you are experiencing frustration in your work.

Shower To dream of taking a shower may symbolize a spiritual renewal. It might also signify a bonus or reward showered upon the dreamer.

Sickness/ Illness If you dream of being ill, ask yourself if you're in need of being cared for and pampered. This dream might also be a message to watch your health. To dream of a family member who is sick represents some misfortune or issue that is troubling your domestic life.

Singing Hearing singing in a dream signifies a pleasant and cheerful attitude and that you may hear promising news over a matter at hand. If you are singing in the dream, note the type (happy, sad) of song you are singing.

Skating Dreaming of skating may signify to the dreamer that they are gliding over a matter at hand, or that they may be skating on thin ice. Note all the aspects of the dream.

Skull To dream of a skull and crossbones is a traditional sign of danger and possibly death—a warning.

Sky Dreaming of the sky symbolizes hope, vitality, and a creative force.

Smoke If you dream of smoke filling a room, it suggests that a matter at hand is being obscured. On the other hand, if the smoke is clearing, clarity is imminent.

Snake A snake is an archetypal image that can have numerous interpretations. In mythology, snakes are symbols of wisdom, of healing and fertility, and—in the shedding of skin—of renewal. Snakes can also symbolize the dangers of the underworld. In Christianity, the snake symbolizes temptation and the source of evil. In some Eastern traditions, the snake is related to a power that rises from the base of the spine and can be a symbol of transformation. The Freudian interpretation relates snakes to the male genitalia. How you view snakes symbolically and other aspects of the dream should guide you in your interpretation.

Snow Snow can represent purity if seen in a pristine landscape. Since snow is a solidified form of water, it can also stand for frozen emotions. If the snow is melting, the suggestion is that frozen feelings are thawing. To find yourself in a snowstorm may represent uncertainty in an emotional matter, or sorrow in failing to enjoy some long expected pleasure. Dreaming of snow-capped mountains in the distance suggests that your ambitions will yield no advancement. Eating snow symbolizes a failure to realize ideals.

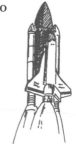

Spaceship A spaceship in a dream may suggest a journey into the unknown, or symbolize a spiritual quest.

Spear Thrusting a spear at someone in a dream may represent an effort to thrust your will on another person. If the spear is hurled over a field, toward a mountain, or an ocean, the dream may mean that you are making a powerful statement to the world.

Spider Spiders may symbolize a careful and energetic approach to your work and that you will be pleasantly rewarded for your

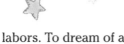

labors. To dream of a spider spinning its web signifies that your homelife will be happy and secure, while many spiders represent good health and friends. A confrontation with a large spider may signify a quick ascent to fame and fortune, unless the large spider bites you, in which it may represent the loss of money or reputation.

Squirrel To see these friendly creatures may mean that pleasant acquaintances will soon visit, or that you will advance in business.

Stairs Climbing a stairway in a dream can mean that you are on your way to achieving a goal. Descending a stairs, or falling down one, might indicate a fall in prestige or economic status. To sit on a step could suggest that you are pausing in your everyday life with its challenges to consider where things stand.

Statue Dreaming of a statue or statues could signify a lack of movement in your life. Statues are also cold and can symbolize frozen feelings.

Stillborn To dream of a stillborn infant indicates a premature ending or some distressing circumstance in a matter at hand.

Stones Stones can represent small irritations or obstacles that must be overcome. Seeing yourself throw a stone in a dream may mean that you have cause to reprove someone.

A circle has been divided into twelve equal parts, each part represents an aspect of life. Outside of each part, write two observations about patterns pertaining to that part of your life. The twelve areas are:

The self: the physical body and your feelings about your body, as well as how you project yourself to others.

Finances: Money. Possessions and earning ability.

Siblings: Brothers and sisters. If you're an only child, then this area pertains to people who are like siblings to you.

Mother and home: all things related to your relationship with your mother and to your home.

Children and creativity: This part includes any creative pursuit, regardless of whether you make money at it.

Health and work: If you're involved in charity work, include it here.

Partnerships: all close partnerships—romantic, business, etc.

(continued)

Sexuality: how you feel about yourself sexually.

Spiritual beliefs: everything pertaining to religious, philosophical, and spiritual beliefs goes here.

Father and profession: all things related to your relationship with your father and to your feelings about your profession and career.

Friends and associates: the people around you, the people you work with, and the groups and associations you belong to all go here.

Dreams, hopes, and wishes: all that you wish to attain.

Once you've completed your comments, focus on those that seem negative or that make you uncomfortable. Then, go to Exercise 8, rewrite them in a positive way.

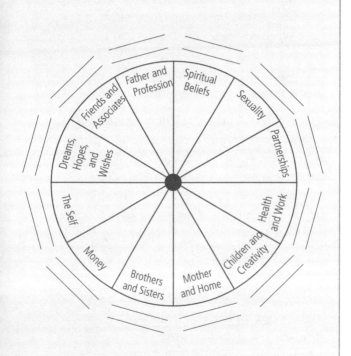

Storm To dream of an approaching storm indicates emotional turmoil in some aspect of your life. Dark skies and thunder may also be a forewarning that danger is approaching. Alternately, a storm could symbolize rapid changes occurring in your life.

Suicide A dream of killing yourself probably is a symbolic reflection of what's going on in your conscious life. Such a dream might reflect a personal transformation, a divorce, changing careers, or other major life shifts. You are essentially killing your past, becoming a new person.

Sun Dreaming of the sun is usually fortuitous. The sun is the symbol of light, warmth, and energy. In Native American lore, the sun symbolizes the father or the masculine principal.

Swimming A dream of swimming suggests the dreamer is immersed in an exploration of emotional matters or the unconscious.

Sword A sword is a symbol of strength and power. It also can cut to the bone. Dreaming of a sword might suggest that aggressive action is required.

T

Table To dream of an empty table might suggest a concern about a lack or shortage of possessions, while a table covered with food may symbolize a time of abundance.

Tamborine The appearance of a tamborine symbolizes pleasure in some unusual undertaking about to take place.

Tattoo Tattoos are associated with the strange and exotic. To dream of seeing your body tattooed suggests that some difficulty will cause you to make a long absence from home or familiar surroundings. Dreaming that you are a tattooist suggests that your desire for some strange experience may alienate you from friends.

Teeth Teeth are what you use to bite. If you lose your bite, you lose power. Losing teeth might also symbolize a loss of face. It could also be a metaphor for "loose" or careless speech. Note the other aspects of the dream. For example, to examine your teeth suggests that you exercise caution in a matter at hand. To clean your teeth represents that some struggle is necessary to keep your standing. Admiring your teeth for their whiteness suggests that wishes for a pleasant occu-

pation and happiness will be fulfilled. To dream
that you pull your own teeth and are feeling
around the cavity with your tongue signifies
your trepidation over a situation about to be
entered into. Dreaming of imperfect teeth is
one of the worst dreams to have for it connotes bad feelings about your appearance and
well-being.

Telephone A telephone might symbolize the attempt to contact the unconscious. If the phone is ringing and no one
is answering, the dream might suggest
that you are ignoring the call of your
unconscious.

Tent A tent provides shelter and is
usually associated with camping. A dream
of a tent could indicate that you are in need of
a getaway, a retreat from everyday life.

Thaw Thawing represents the rebirth or return to pleasant conditions. To dream of seeing ice thaw may symbolize that something or someone that was giving you trouble will soon yield pleasure and profit.

The President of the United States Not as uncommon as it may seem, to talk with the President of the United States in a dream may represent an interest in lofty ideals or political matters, or a strong desire to be a politician.

Thief If you dream of someone stealing something, the implication is that something is being taken from you. It could be a boss or colleague who is stealing your energy or ideas, rather than an actual theft of goods. If you're the thief, the message may be a warning that you are taking what you don't deserve and that you should change your ways.

Thirst A dream in which you are thirsty suggests that you are in need of nourishment, either physical, mental, or emotional. To see others relieving their thirst suggests that this nourishment may come from others.

Thorn A thorn may represent an annoyance of some sort, "a thorn in your side."

Tiger Aggressive and fierce in the wild, to see these animals in your dream may symbolize that you are under persecution or will be tormented. However, if you see yourself fending off an attack, this may mean that you will be extremely successful in all your ventures.

Tornado Swift and terrible agents of destruction in nature, a dream involving a tornado suggests that your desire for a quick resolution in a matter at hand may lead to disappointment.

Torrent To dream of a seething torrent of water suggests a profound unrest in the emotional state of the dreamer or a person in the dream.

Tower To dream of a tower could symbolize vigilance, as a watchtower, or punishment or isolation as a guard tower. Dreaming of being in an "ivory tower" indicates that you or the subject of your dream is out of touch with the everyday world.

Train A train symbolizes a journey. Look at the other elements in the dream to understand the nature of your journey. If the train isn't moving, the dream might be suggesting some impediment in your life. If you can't find your luggage, the dream might indicate that

you are concerned that you're not ready for this journey. If you are on a smoothly running train, but there are no tracks, the dream might signify that you are concerned over some affair that will eventually be resolved satisfactorily. Traveling on the wrong train may indicate your journey is in need of a correction.

Treasure A dream of a treasure may suggests a hidden talent or hidden abilities that you can now unearth. It could indicate latent psychic abilities.

Tree A tree is a symbol of strength and foundation. It may also symbolize inner strength. A tree exists both below the earth and above it. In that sense, a tree transcends the sky above and the earth below and stands for the realms of

nature and the spirit. To dream of a tree in new foliage represents a pleasant outcome to your hopes and desires. Tree-climbing dreams may signify a quick ascent in business. Green trees newly felled augur unexpected unhappiness after a period of prosperity and delight.

Trial A dream of being on trial suggests that you are being judged, or are afraid of being judged. Alternately, a trial in a dream could indicate that you are judging others too harshly.

Triplets To dream of triplets indicates success in a matter where failure was feared. For a man to dream of his wife having triplets represents a pleasing end to a situation that has long been in dispute. To hear newly born triplets crying suggests a disagreement that will soon be resolved in your favor.

Tunnel From a Freudian perspective, a dream of a tunnel suggests a vagina, and a train entering the tunnel represents sexual intercourse. A tunnel may also be a link between two conditions: When you exit the tunnel, you will enter a new state of mind.

Turtle While dreaming of a turtle might symbolize slow, painstaking movement, the shelled creature is also a symbol of spiritual development.

Twins A dream of twins may mean that there are two parts to a matter of concern or two aspects to your personality. Seeing twins in a dream symbolizes security in a business matter and faithfulness in a domestic issue.

U

Umbrella An umbrella represents protection against adverse conditions or an emotional flood from the unconscious. If the umbrella is closed and you're being soaked by a downpour, the indication is that you are open to your emotional needs.

Underground To dream of being in an underground habitation often symbolizes contact with your subconscious. Other images in the dream will provide more meaning to the nature of the contact. Is there something you've been hiding here that should be brought to the "surface"? Ask yourself how you feel about the situation. Do you feel protected by the underground cavern or room? Or are you being held prisoner or hiding? Dreaming of an underground railway could indicate passage to another state of being, a

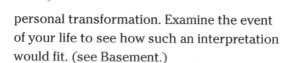

personal transformation. Examine the event of your life to see how such an interpretation would fit. (see Basement.)

Underwear A dream of underwear may symbolize that you are exposing something that is under cover or hidden. It could indicate that you're bringing matters from the unconscious to the surface.

Unicycle If you are riding a unicycle in a dream, you may be concerned about balance. Alternately, you're the "big wheel" and on your own.

United States Mailbox A mailbox is a symbol of authority; consequently, putting a letter in a mailbox may mean you are submitting to authority, or feeling guilt over a particular matter.

Urination A dream in which you urinate may simply indicate that you need to wake up and go to the bathroom. Symbolically, the dream may indicate a desire to eliminate impurities from your life.

V

Vagrant Are you afraid of losing your home, stability, or livelihood? Perhaps you want to break away from social regimentation.

Valuables Uncovering valuables may symbolize the discovery of self-worth or inner resources.

Vampire To dream of a vampire may indicate that someone is draining energy from you or taking advantage of you. The message is to guard against people who take too much of your time or energy. To dream of battling or staking a vampire suggests a positive outcome versus someone with harmful intentions.

Vault A vault usually holds valuables. Your ability to open it determines the nature of the dream. If you hold the key, the vault may be a symbol of wealth and prosperity. If you are unable to open it, then the dream may signify that you are being frustrated in your effort to achieve wealth or a specific goal.

Veil A dream in which someone or something is veiled suggests that you're hiding something or something is being hidden from you.

Victim A dream of yourself as a victim may indicate that you're feeling helpless regarding a situation. If someone rescues you, the dream suggests that help is available.

Violin A violin played in a dream portends a romantic interlude, a time of love and harmony. It can also mean that you or someone else is "high strung."

Visitor Encountering a visitor in a dream indicates that a new condition is entering your life. If you welcome the visitor, the change may be for the better. If you turn away the visitor, you're unwilling to change or you don't accept what is being offered.

Volcano The eruption of a volcano or a smoking volcano may suggest that your strong emotions are rising to the surface and need to be expressed before you literally explode.

Vomit To vomit in a dream may be a dramatic exhibition of a need to rid something or someone from your life. To dream of vomitting a chicken suggests an illness in a relative will be a cause of disappointment. To see others vomitting symbolizes that someone's false pretenses will soon be made apparent.

Wallet A wallet carries personal effects, such as your identification. It is also where you carry financial resources. If you dream of losing your wallet, it may relate to a concern about your sense of self or about your finances. What happens in the dream and how you react can help you determine its meaning.

War A dream of war could relate to reliving your past in the military. Whether you've served in the military or not, a dream of war might symbolize internal turmoil or a need to make peace with yourself, or others. By examining other elements in the dream, you may determine the message behind the aggressive behavior.

Washing If you are washing something in a dream, you may be attempting to cleanse or purify the self. If a stain won't come out, the dream may relate to a concern about something from your past connected with feelings of guilt.

Water A dream of water can relate to the emotions or the unconscious. In the Freudian perspective, water relates to sexual matters, usually the female genitalia. (see Lake, Ocean, River, and Waves.)

Waterfall Water signifies the unconscious or the emotions, so to dream of waterfalls may represent a sudden or dramatic change in the dreamer's emotional state.

Waves Waves symbolize the power of the unconscious or emotions. Enormous breaking waves may represent powerful emotions, and gentle waves may suggest a tranquil state of mind.

Weapon Weapons may stand for the male genitals. The meaning of the dream is best determined by considering who is holding the weapon and how it is being used.

Wedding Weddings are a union between two people, and dreams of weddings may symbolize the joining or acceptance of your

Wind, Gales

Dreaming of wind softly blowing signifies you will receive a considerable inheritance from a beloved one. Although you experience sadness over the death of this loved one, you will know happiness in the future.

If you dream you are walking against a brisk wind, it indicates you are courageous, resist temptations, and pursue your hopes with a plucky determination. You will be successful. If, however, in your dream the wind blows you along against your wishes, it signifies you might have disappointments in love and in business.

If, of all things, you dream you are caught in a gale, watch out—you might have business losses.

unconscious to an idea or emotion. To attend a wedding in a dream connotes an occasion that may bring about bitterness and delayed success. To dream of a wedding that is not approved by your parents suggests unrest among family members over a situation.

Weeds Dreaming of weeds suggests that something needs to be weeded out from your life. An overgrown garden might signify that something is being neglected in your life.

Well A well in a dream reveals that resources are available deep within you, although you may not be aware of it. To fall into a well symbolizes a loss of control regarding a matter at hand. A dry well indicates that you feel a part of your life is empty and needs to be nourished. To draw water from a well denotes the fulfillment of ardent desires.

Wet As in the saying "you're all wet," wetness represents uncertainty or a lack of knowledge. Maybe someone is giving you bad advice for a particular situation. For a young woman to dream that she is soaking wet symbolizes a disgraceful affair with someone who is already attached.

Whale A whale is an enormous mammal and to dream of one might indicate that you are dealing with a whale of a project. On the other hand, a whale dream may suggest you are overwhelmed. Whales can also relate to water and the relationship of the self to the unconscious and the emotions.

Whirlpool Water represents the emotions or the unconscious, so to dream of a whirlpool may indicate that your emotions are in a state of flux and can ensnarl you unless caution is exercised.

Whirlwind A dream of a whirlwind suggests that you are confronting a change in a matter at hand which threatens to overwhelm you. Pay attention to the other aspects of the dream. Are you facing this danger alone or with somebody? Are you in your house?

Window If a window appears in a dream, it may symbolize a view of your life from the inside out. Are there changes you would like to make? If the view is illuminated, then the outlook is bright. If you are on the outside looking in, you may feel that you have been excluded from something.

Wine Drinking wine in a dream might be a sign of celebration. It can also represent an elevated or altered state of mind. In a spiritual sense, wine can symbolize a transformation. For an alcoholic or someone who has been affected by one, wine or other alcoholic beverages can represent a negative influence.

Wings Wings are a means of transport and they may suggest that you will soar to wealth and honor, or that you are worried over someone who has gone on a long journey.

Witch How one sees a witch determines the meaning of a dream in which one appears. The Halloween image of a witch might be symbolic of a scary or evil scenario. For those involved in Wicca or attracted to New Age ideas, a witch might relate to the worship and respect of nature and the earth.

Wolf In Native American lore, the wolf is good medicine, a symbol of the pathfinder, a teacher with great wisdom and

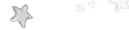

knowledge. Dreaming of a wolf can be auspicious. Alternately, the wolf can be a symbol of a lone male aggressively pursuing a young female as in the Little Red Riding Hood fable.

Woman The appearance of different types of women can symbolize different things in a dream. A dark-haired woman with blue eyes and a pug nose may represent a withdrawal from a matter at hand. A brown-eyed woman with a hook nose may suggest that you will be lured into a speculative venture. A woman who appears with auburn hair only adds to your anxiety over an issue. A blonde woman is symbolic of a favorable or pleasing outcome.

Writing Writing is usually difficult to read in a dream, so the message is usually symbolic. Writing could serve as a warning as in "the handwriting is on the wall." Writing could also suggest that your inner self is seeking to make contact with your conscious self. Ancient writings in a dream indicate that the dreamer is seeking knowledge from the distant past.

Yard Dreaming of a yard may relate to your childhood, a time when you played in the yard. The dream may symbolize a longing for a carefree time, for more personal space, or for something to fill the vacancy of the yard.

Yellow In the positive sense, yellow is the symbol of brightness, energy, and intellect. The color can also be linked to cowardice behavior.

Youth A dream of a youth might signify that you are being energized by those younger than you. Seeing yourself as younger in a dream may point to youthful self-empowerment.

Z

Zero A symbol of many interpretations, zero can mean emptiness, a lack of something in your life. It also forms a circle and can stand for wholeness and completion, or even the mysteries of the unknown. In Freudian terms, the shape is reminiscent of a vagina and suggests a desire for sexual relations.

Zoo A dream of a zoo might relate to a feeling of being in a cage. It could also symbolize chaos as in "The place is like a zoo." Alternately, it could recall a time of recreation, relaxation, and pleasure.

EXERCISE 8: MY PATTERNS

Once you've completed your comments in Exercise 7, focus on those that seem negative or that make you uncomfortable. Then rewrite them here in a positive way.

Patterns I want to create

Self: _____

Money: _____

Brothers and sisters: _____

Mother and home: _____

Children and creativity: _____

Health and work: _____

Partnerships: _____

Sexuality: _____

Spiritual beliefs: _____

Father and profession: _____

(continued)

EXERCISE 8: MY PATTERNS

Friends and associates: _____

Dreams, hopes and wishes: _____

Notes:

_____

_____

_____

_____

_____

_____

_____

_____

_____

_____

_____